DRAW IT HAPPY!

100+ FUNNY ANIMALS AND FANTASTIC CHARACTERS

Terry Runyan

QUARRY

CONTENTS

Introduction 3

Characters

Animals

INTRODUCTION

I'm kind of obsessed with drawing animals. As a kid I primarily drew horses and dogs, but as I continued to create more illustrations, particularly for myself, cats became a dominant theme. I've also always considered myself a character artist of sorts. Most of the time something feels missing if there isn't a character in the mix. Because of these two factors, I love creating fun stories with characters, and of course making them cute!

Use this book as a guide and reference to develop your own unique characters and animals. Use the steps to learn about and practice each subject's basic shapes and characteristics. You can start with the facial features—eyes, nose, and mouth—then work your way through the drawing, adding details and other features to make the character unique. You can add the head shape, ears, body shape, and clothing or distinguishing marks. Once you have the basic shapes and details down, try drawing the animal or character in different variations and situations, then maybe add some friends to help tell a story.

Although I created the drawings in this book digitally, I recommend that you try as many mediums as you can—pencils, colored pencils, crayons, pens, cut paper, paints, and digital platforms—to see which are most fun for you. This kind of exploration will help you develop your own style of drawing.

Remember, taking time to draw often, even daily, is the best way to become more skilled at drawing. Giving yourself time to draw makes all the difference, not only in improving your skills but in igniting your creativity. Drawing is a wonderful way to experiment, have fun, and enjoy a bit of happy!

DRAW A BASEBALL BAT

DRAW A SUPERHERO SLOTH

DRAW A SWEET TOOTH

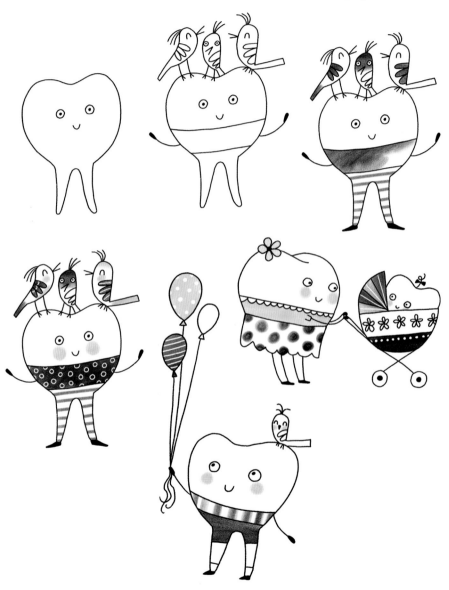

DRAW A BEACH BUM

DRAW A TEA TIMER

TIP
Characters come to life with a smile and a sweet friend. Also, mixing up patterns and shapes is a great way to add variety to your cups!

DRAW A BIRD WATCHER

DRAW A PARTY MONSTER

DRAW A FELINE FASHIONISTA

DRAW A DRUM MAJOR

DRAW A BABYSITTER

DRAW A FRUIT LOVER

DRAW AN OFFICE MONKEY

DRAW A TIPSY TUMBLER

DRAW AN AIRY FAIRY

DRAW A BUSY BEAVER

TIP

How would a human work on the job? What equipment and supplies do they use? Answering questions like these while drawing a busy beaver can make for a happy workplace.

DRAW A FAST FOODIE

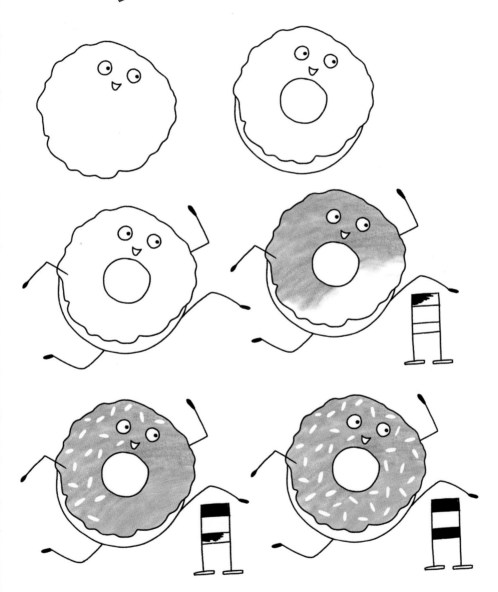

DRAW A MINI MAGICIAN

DRAW A NIGHT OWL

DRAW A CLASSROOM CHARACTER

DRAW A DINO DUDE

DRAW A GHOST WRITER

DRAW A COUCH POTATO

DRAW A MOVIE STAR

DRAW A SEA LION

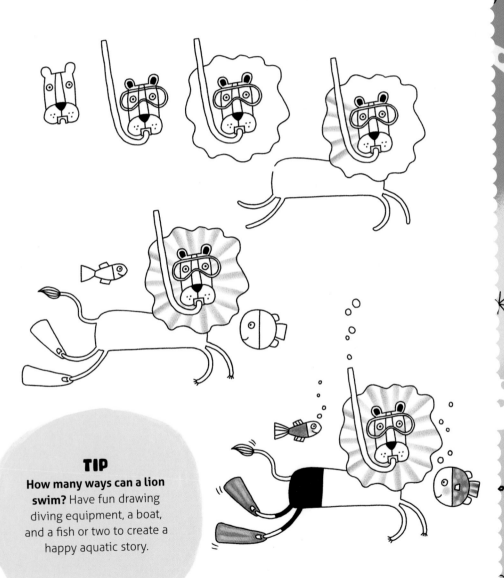

TIP
How many ways can a lion swim? Have fun drawing diving equipment, a boat, and a fish or two to create a happy aquatic story.

DRAW A VEGGIE INGENUE

DRAW A DOG WALKER

DRAW A ROBOT NERD

DRAW A LOVEY DOVE

DRAW A PLANT TENDER

DRAW A FLYING PIG

DRAW A GOOD EGG

DRAW A GLEE FROG

DRAW A BEACHCOMBER

DRAW A POT HEAD

DRAW A SPACE ODDITY

DRAW A HOBBY HORSE

TIP
The possibilities are endless when it comes to hobbies!
Pick an animal and a hobby and get your animal creating.

DRAW A CAT BURGLAR

DRAW A SWEETIE PIE

DRAW A WILD GOOSE

DRAW A CACTUS COWBOY

DRAW A LAB RAT

DRAW A ZEN GOUDA

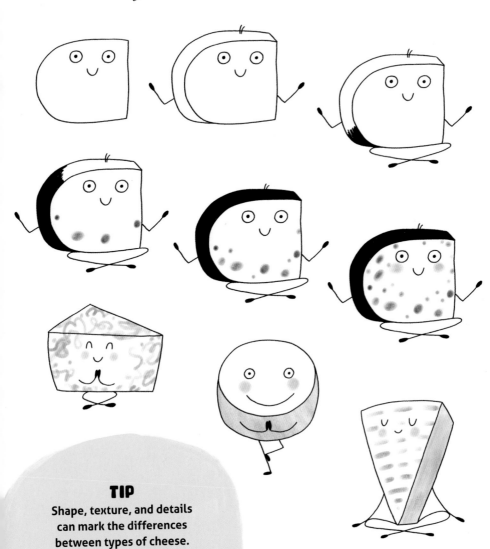

TIP
**Shape, texture, and details
can mark the differences
between types of cheese.**
How they meditate and do yoga
can make them very zen.

DRAW A VAMPIRE ACROBAT

DRAW A COUNTING SHEEP

TIP
Counting is something accountants, bankers, and insomniacs often do. Think about the situations in which people count and add your characters to them.

DRAW A FIBER FANATIC

DRAW A BOOKWORM

DRAW A SKATE DATE

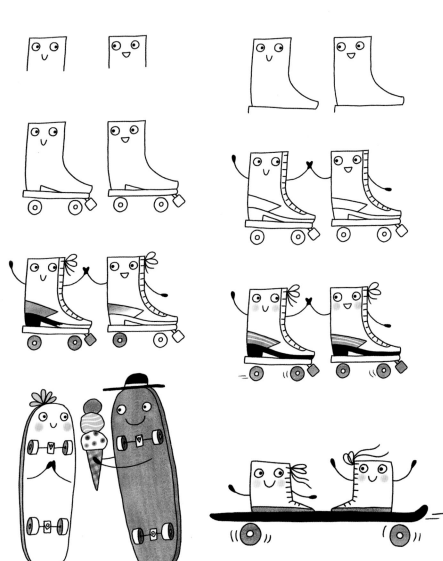

DRAW AN ANT IN PANTS

DRAW A TINY PLANET

DRAW A TURKEY TROTTER

DRAW A COFFEE BEING

DRAW A SHERLOCK GNOME

DRAW A TOP BANANA

DRAW A MUSTACHE MAN

DRAW A DONUT OFFICER

DRAW AN EARLY BIRD

DRAW A PEACHY QUEEN

DRAW AN UNI-CYCLIST

DRAW A HE-MAN MAILMAN

DRAW A WINE CONNOISSEUR

DRAW A TOUGH COOKIE

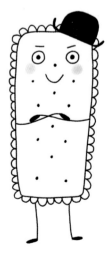

DRAW A DRAMATIC FLARE

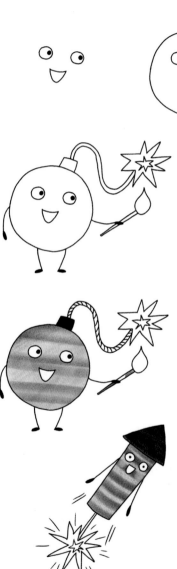

TIP

Nothing says surprise like large round eyes with the pupils in the middle. To soften the emotion, move the pupils off-center a bit (or a lot), and make the outer shape of the eyes smaller.

DRAW A GUINEA PIG

DRAW A WALRUS

DRAW A CHAMELEON

DRAW A SPOTTED DOG

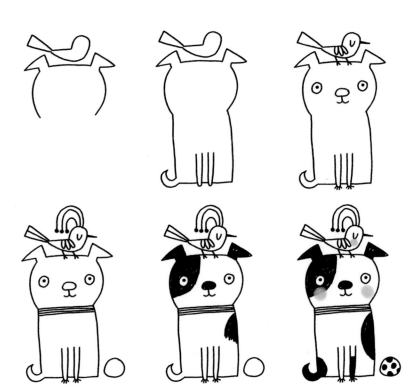

DRAW A MOUNTAIN GOAT

TIP
When creating happy animals, try adding baby animals into the mix, or a bird or two. Having animals interact with each other can create a happy story.

DRAW A HERMIT CRAB

DRAW AN IGUANA

DRAW A FRUIT BAT

DRAW A LION

DRAW A BACKYARD BIRD

DRAW A FERRET

DRAW A BUTTERFLY

DRAW A SIFAKA LEMUR

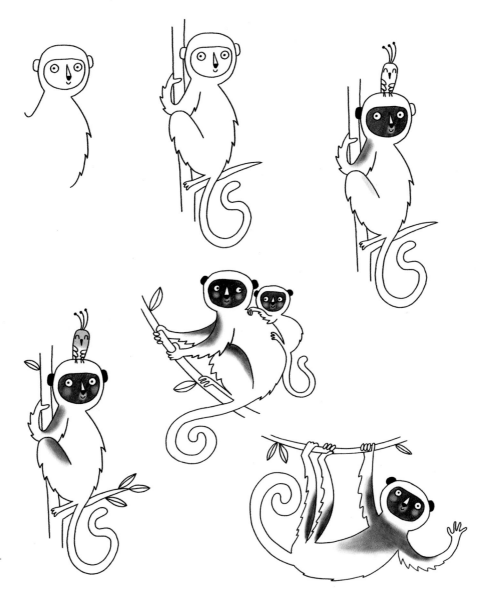

DRAW A ZEBRA

DRAW A BEAVER

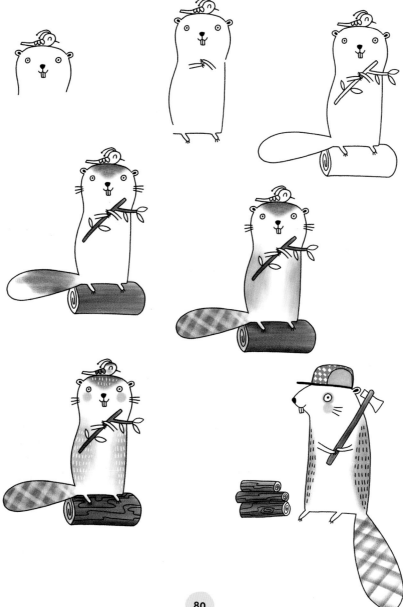

DRAW A FISH

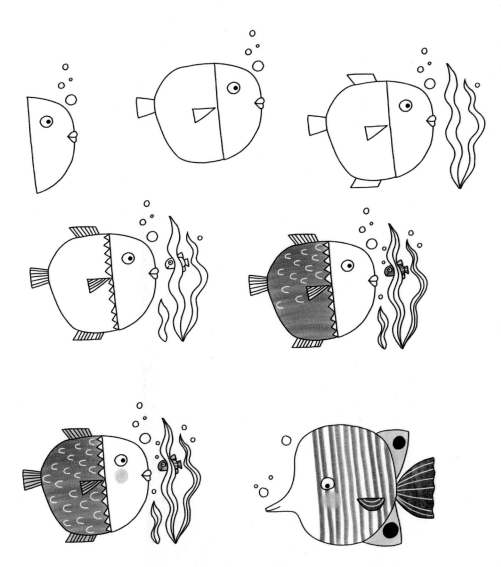

DRAW AN ALLIGATOR

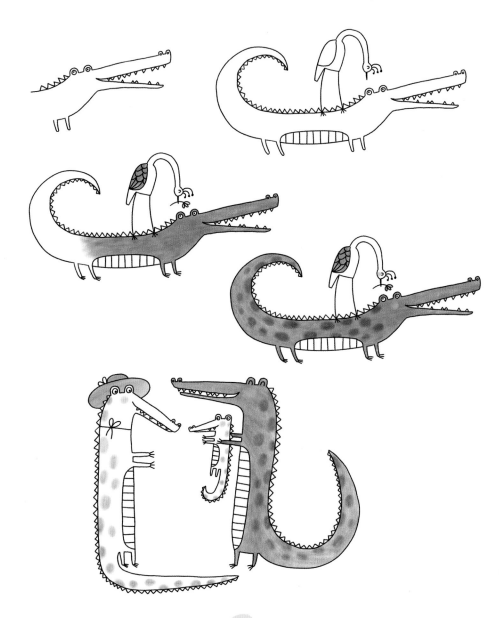

DRAW A MANED WOLF

DRAW A PIGEON

DRAW A YAK

DRAW A DOLPHIN

DRAW A FROG

DRAW A RACCOON

DRAW A COZY CAT

DRAW A POLAR BEAR

TIP
The animal's habitat can make your drawing even more recognizable and **fun!** Add an iceberg and a penguin, and your polar bear has a party!

DRAW A TASMANIAN DEVIL

DRAW A RAM

DRAW A BUNNY

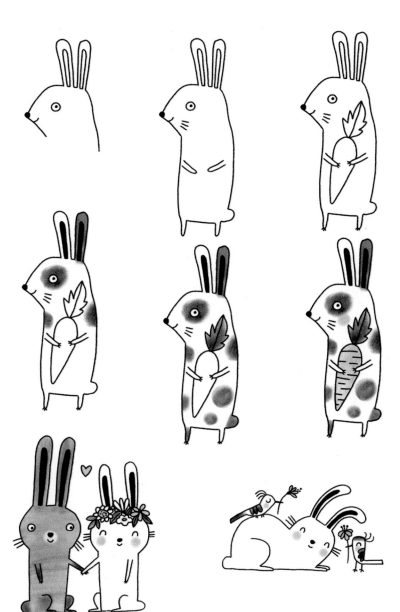

DRAW A SPIDER

DRAW A CHEETAH

DRAW AN ANTEATER

DRAW AN ORANGUTAN

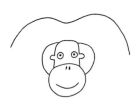

TIP

Animals with long hair are fun to draw.
Use the side of a pencil to lay the hair down in the direction it falls. Also, orangutans have hands like humans. They're great at holding ice cream cones and hanging from branches.

DRAW AN IMPALA

DRAW A CRAB

TIP
Adding little details like a bowtie, shoes, or hat can really add character to a drawing.
A little book and a bowtie can make a crab look rather sophisticated.

DRAW A MONGOOSE

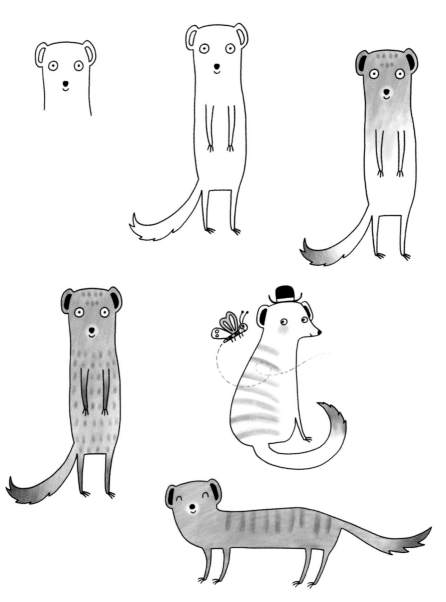

DRAW A NEWT

DRAW A PARROT

DRAW A WILD DOG

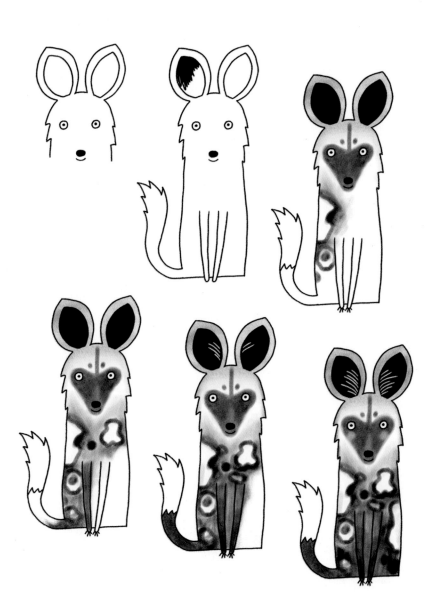

DRAW A HORSE

DRAW A BINTURONG

DRAW A LIZARD

DRAW A DESIGNER DOG

DRAW A MONKEY

DRAW A HAMSTER

DRAW A LUNA MOTH

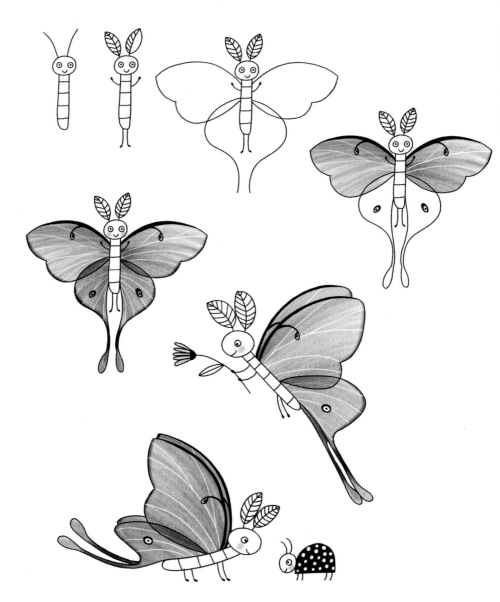

DRAW A BUSH BABY

DRAW A MOOSE

TIP

The shape of the eyes says a lot about how your animal is feeling. An upside-down U shape is a happy eye, while a right side up U can mean the animal is looking down or is sleepy.

DRAW A SPOTTED GENET

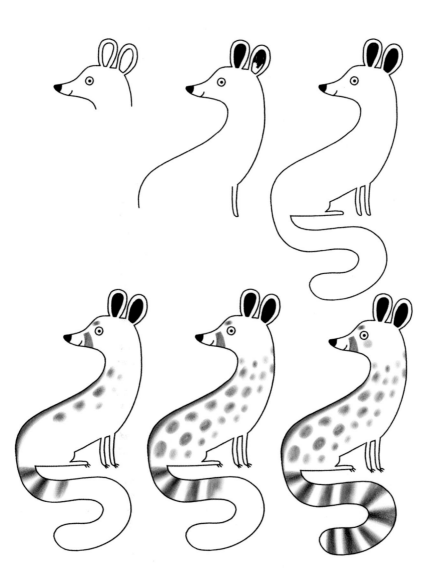

DRAW A COW

DRAW A SNAKE

DRAW AN EMU

DRAW A NUMBAT

DRAW AN OKAPI

DRAW A BUSY CAT

DRAW A HOOPOE BIRD

DRAW A PECCARY

DRAW A FENNEC FOX

DRAW AN ASIAN BLACK BEAR

DRAW A PORCUPINE

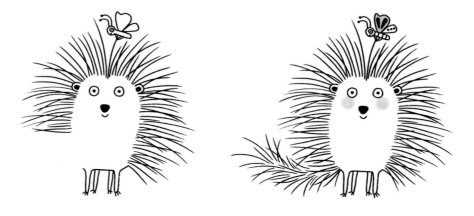

DRAW A LYNX

DRAW A RHINO

DRAW A LONG-EARED JERBOA

TIP
Try adding cute details to your animals to give them more personality. Matching scarves can show friendship between animals. And what animal can't be happy with a little heart to hold?

About the Author

Terry Runyan is a visual artist and creative encourager. After a long career as an in-house illustrator for Hallmark, Runyan now runs her own business, creating art and videos, presenting webinars, and leading classes to help others explore their creativity. She loves all animals, and her artwork usually includes a gathering of furry, feathery, and fishy friends. She works in a variety of mediums, including paint, collage, drawing, digital, and video. She lives in Leawood, Kansas. To see more of her work, visit her website: www.terryrunyan.com.

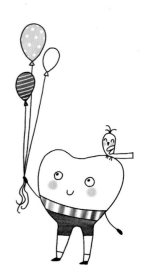

Quarto.com
© 2024 Quarto Publishing Group USA Inc.
Illustrations © 2020 Terry Runyan

First Published in 2024 by Quarry Books, an imprint of The Quarto Group,
100 Cummings Center, Suite 265-D, Beverly, MA 01915, USA.
T (978) 282-9590 F (978) 283-2742

Quarry Books titles are also available at discount for retail, wholesale, promotional, and bulk purchase.

For details, contact the Special Sales Manager by email at specialsales@quarto.com or by mail at The Quarto Group, Attn: Special Sales Manager, 100 Cummings Center, Suite 265-D, Beverly, MA 01915, USA.

10 9 8 7 6 5 4 3 2 1

ISBN: 978-0-7603-9238-6

Digital edition published in 2024
eISBN: 978-0-7603-9239-3

The content in this book previously appeared in *Draw 62 Animals and Make Them Happy* and *Draw 62 Characters and Make Them Happy* both published by Quarry Books in 2020 and written and illustrated by Terry Runyan.

Library of Congress Cataloging-in-Publication Data available

Design: Evelin Kasikov
Illustration: Terry Runyan

Printed in China